Later

Sarah Tanksley

BookLeaf Publishing

India | USA | UK

Presentation by *BookLeaf Publishing*

Web: www.bookleafpub.com

E-mail: info@bookleafpub.com

ISBN:9789360941864

First edition 2024

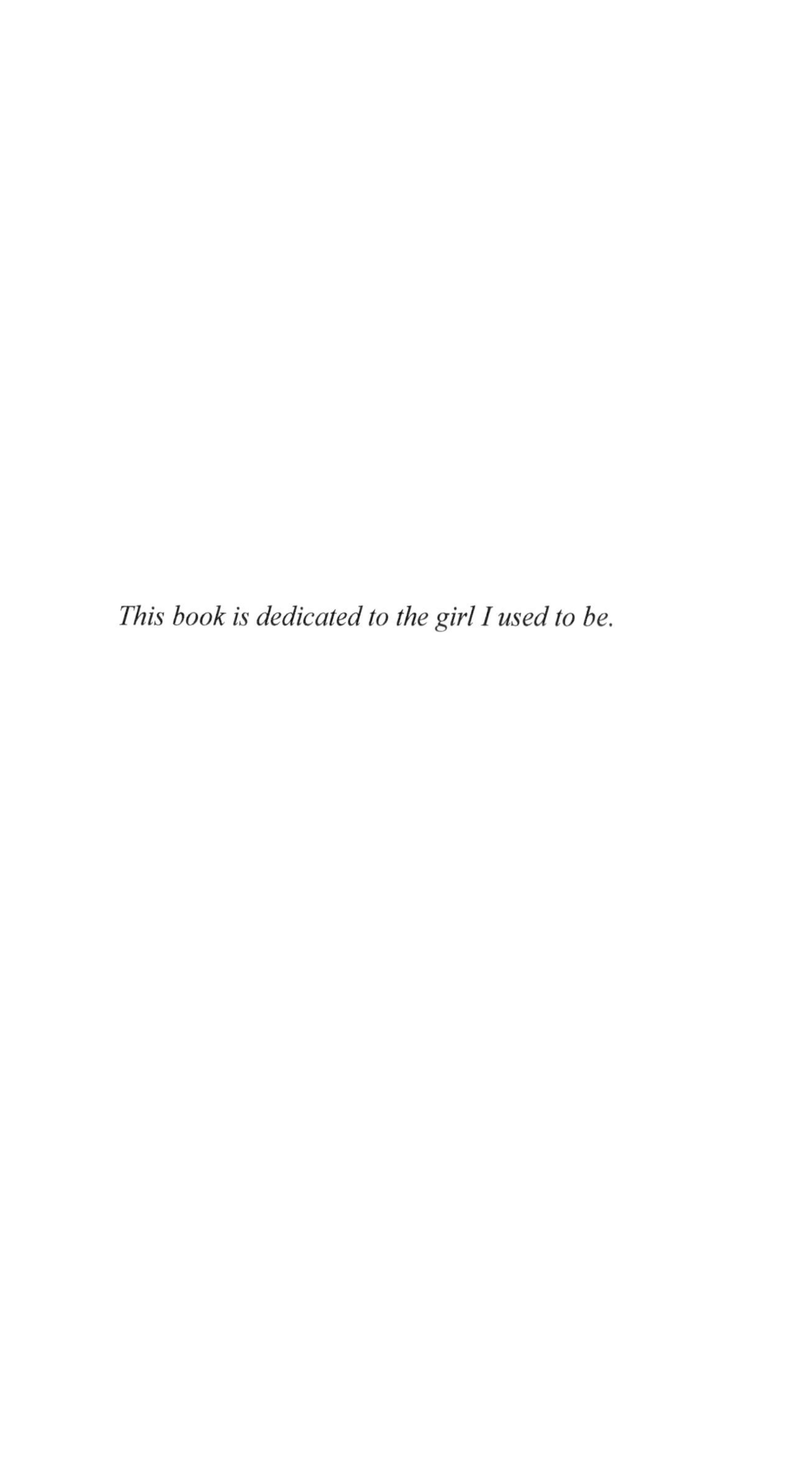

This book is dedicated to the girl I used to be.

PREFACE

I haven't written in years. At some point, I decided that no one would want to read my words, and then, eventually, I believed that I didn't have any words to say.
Watching my daughter struggle to find her voice has forced me to rediscover my own. How could I encourage her to speak up for herself when I am not willing to put the work in myself?
And so I am writing, in fits and starts, which, fortunately, can work for poetry. This short book is the first draft, the first hint of the story that urgently wants to be told.

Not Much

I'm not much of a poet
Or a writer anymore
Ideas sometimes come
But when pen hits paper they fade
Like a dream you strain to remember
Only for a few seconds
While stretching awake
I am writing these poems
Because I am fragmented
Like these phrases
And I cannot make sentences anymore

The Ex

He is a cancer
Just when my body relaxes
Thinking he's finally gone for good
He reminds me that he can return
And kill me at any time.

Panic Rises

Panic rises
From my tightening chest
And reddens my face
My body quivers, then shakes
When I hear his name
Or his voice
Or if I imagine his sneer,
The uneven curl of his upper lip, a precursor to his
vitriol
The hate in him metastasizing
Lethal to the soul of anyone in his path

Poison Gas

I have words I desperately need to speak
Stories that urgently must be told
But my thoughts dissipate in my head
Like a vapor
A poisonous vapor that won't condense back into
words
And so the stories
That are begging to be shared
Will absorb into my body
People will ask me
Why are you trembling?
And I will try to explain about the poison gas

The Right

I long to feel free from you
The angry vitriol spilling from your mouth
Like bullets firing from a weapon
That has been loaded and waiting for me
A long time
And the stealth attacks to scare me
To make me question my own rational mind
Am I in danger now?
Yes . . . no . . . yes

People shake their heads and say
That's too bad, I'm sorry
But I am not going to help you
You don't deserve it, but maybe it is your fault
Choices have consequences, you know

But then I remember
That so many lives are silenced
By acts of targeted violence
By acts of random violence
By disease, by accidents
By starvation, genocide, atrocities that other people
could prevent
But don't
So why do I believe
I have the right
To feel safe
To survive
To thrive?

In Perpetuity

This must be an affectation
I thought
I didn't believe such cruelty
Could stand before me
Looking so true
He is young, I thought
Young and lovely
He will grow out of it
He doesn't mean it when he says
That if he ever committed suicide
He would haul his AR-15 to a gay bar
And take a bunch of them with him
That is pain, I thought
Not evil
I can fix this
I took a gamble
And spun the wheel
And lost
And must pay
With my peace
In perpetuity

I'm Ready

I'm ready to be old
Ready to sit in a chair and read
Through eyeglasses that dangle from a chain
Around my neck
Until I place them on the tip of my nose
With my dog curled and pressed beside me

When I walk
I will move slowly
Like I'm walking through syrup
But I won't care
I will walk anyway, for hours

I'm ready to shout "speak up" into the phone
Ready to shrug at the skin falling from my bones
Like chicken
After hours in a slow cooker

I've already seen this world
I already know how this story ends
I'm ready to say
I'm too old for that

Ideal Me

Ideal me
Maintains a home with no clutter on the counters
And no water stains on the shower doors
She exercises first thing, every morning
She doesn't drink coffee or eat processed food
She never dresses from a laundry basket all week
Instead she neatly folds and tucks her clothes into
mahogany drawers
She expects nothing and accepts everything
She is a contemplative judge with measured reactions
Not a mad scientist with a sine wave of emotions

An Abrupt Exit

You were always smiling
In your apartment down the hall
That you purchased, exactly one week after I
purchased mine
This sounds cliche
But you, your smile was like plugging in a Christmas
tree

I would lay on your living room floor, chatting away
You would sit in your chair, grinning, because you
didn't understand the appeal of laying on the floor
We were talking logistics, for what, I don't remember
anymore
Surely one of our endless neighborhood parties

Even before your abrupt exit
I would think of you
As I still do
When I hear the word
Optimist

And you were delighted
With your kind wife, whom you were beginning to
think you'd never find
You sold the unit down the hall
And bought a house in the suburbs
And after that, I only saw you online

And after years of trying
You said, no problem
Let's adopt
Photos of you with a baby boy
Appeared on your page

You went in for a backache
It had been nagging you for over a year
You thought you'd get a referral for physical therapy
And hot massages
But what you got
Was an oncologist instead

Your optimism made way for courage and dignity
I imagine your last words
"I'm so happy I was able to visit here."

Stories

I tell you stories
In desperation
You moan
Not another life lesson Mom
You act like you have no use
For my words
But I know my time is limited
And you will need a heavy toolbox
To rebuild once I am gone
And so I tell you these stories
With an urgency you don't feel

The End of the World

It's not the end of the world
You say
But I might prefer the end of the world
If given the choice between that
And what I must endure now

My Secret

Searching after the tide has receded
Is always best
Especially after a strong storm
Or a full moon
Or both

I find the perfect stick for digging in the rocky sand
Full of frosted glass fragments
Pastels, browns and dollar greens
And remnants of pottery, some still with a pattern
Tumbled terra cotta
The occasional marble worn by water and by time

These treasures, I imagine
Are from cargo carried by the dozens of ships
That wrecked long ago, right off this coast
This is not a beach
This is my secret archeological dig

Forgiveness

I want to forgive you
But I still have so many questions
I still want to hear your answers
So I can tell you why you are so wrong

I still want you to hang your head
And say I'm so sorry, can you ever forgive me
And say I have no answers for how I treated you

So I cannot forgive you
Because forgiveness is moving on
Without answers
And without an apology

After You

One day we were chatting on the phone
The next day you were just gone
Like my favorite lipstick
That was discontinued
I will not ever find that perfect shade
Bringing my face to life
In anyone who comes after you

Sputters

A mind can be a flooded engine
With so much fuel that it chokes on its own thoughts
Before they can become words
And so it only sputters instead of speaks

Sugar and Salt

Some people flavor your life
Like salt
Delectable, even necessary, in small pinches
But deadly in obvious excess
Burning the tongue as a warning

Some people flavor your life
Like sugar
Irresistible, divine, seductive
Almost always welcome
A stealth assassin

The Truth

You won't believe what happened
There must be more to the story
You say
As you cross your arms
Somehow, it must be her fault
Something she did caused this

Because if you accept what happened
You must face the truth
That it could happen to you too

The Party

We were royals holding court
Selecting friends to join our table
Curated for our entertainment

Songs performed in perfect pitch
Dancers breaking on beat
Edgy clothes
Hanging from perfect model bodies
That balance on shoes with painfully sharp heels

The party lasted a decade
Starting and stopping
For workday interruptions
Until some of us grew up
And some of us didn't
Like the lost boys of Peter Pan